Queen ELIZABETH II

Vic Parker

www.raintreepublishers.co.uk
Visit our website to find out more information about Raintree books.

To order:
☎ Phone 0845 6044371
🖹 Fax +44 (0) 1865 312263
✉ Email myorders@raintreepublishers.co.uk

Customers from outside the UK please telephone +44 1865 312262

Raintree is an imprint of Capstone Global Library Limited, a company incorporated in England and Wales having its registered office at 7 Pilgrim Street, London, EC4V 6LB – Registered company number: 6695582

Edited by Louise Galpine and Laura Knowles
Designed by Philippa Jenkins
Picture research by Hannah Taylor and Tracy Cummins
Originated by Capstone Global Library
Printed and bound in China by South China Printing Company

ISBN 978 1 406 24617 9 (paperback)
15 14 13 12 11
10 9 8 7 6 5 4 3 2 1

British Library Cataloguing in Publication Data
Parker, Victoria.
Queen Elizabeth II.
941'.085'092-dc23
A full catalogue record for this book is available from the British Library.

Acknowledgements
We would like to thank the following for permission to reproduce photographs: Camera Press p. **24**; Corbis pp. **8** (Bettmann), **10** (Hulton Deutsch Collection), **22** (Reuters); Getty Images pp. **4**, **6** (Popperfoto), **7** (Popperfoto), **9** (Hulton Archive), **11** (Hulton Archive), **12** (Hulton Archive), **13** (Popperfoto), **14** (Popperfoto), **15** (Roger Viollet), **16** (Hulton Archive), **18** (Hulton Archive), **26** (WireImage/ Anwar Hussein Collection); John Frost newspapers p. **17**; JS Library International p. **19**; Press Association Images pp. **20** (Stefan Rousseau), **21** (Stefan Rousseau), **23** (John Stillwell), **25** (David Cheskin), **27** (AP Photo/Martin Meissner).

Cover photograph of Queen Elizabeth II reproduced with permission of Corbis (Rex Features/Tim Rooke).

Every effort has been made to contact copyright holders of any material reproduced in this book. Any omissions will be rectified in subsequent printings if notice is given to the publisher.

Contents

Some words are printed in bold, **like this**. You can find out what they mean in the glossary.

Who is Queen Elizabeth II?

Elizabeth II (you say, "the Second") is Queen of the **United Kingdom**. She is also head of a group of countries called the **Commonwealth**. Here she is with some Commonwealth leaders.

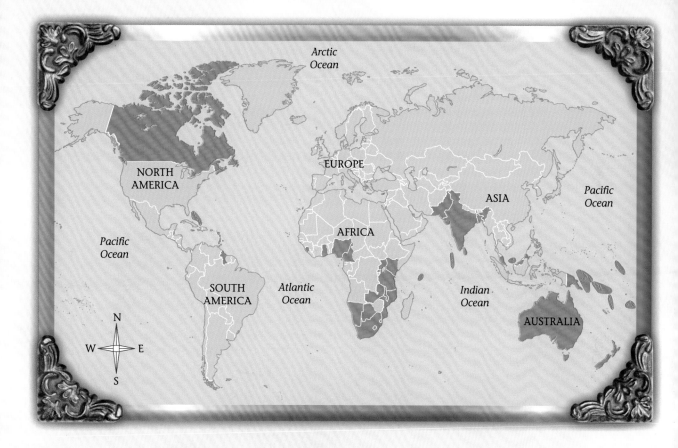

This is a map of the world. The Commonwealth countries are coloured in pink. The United Kingdom is part of the Commonwealth. We call it "the **UK**" for short. It is yellow on this map.

Early years

Elizabeth was born on 21 April 1926. Her grandparents were King and Queen of the **UK**. Her parents were a **duke** and **duchess**. Elizabeth was a princess. Here is Elizabeth and her parents at her **christening**.

When Elizabeth was four years old, her parents had another baby, Margaret. Elizabeth liked looking after her little sister. They all lived in London near the King's home, Buckingham Palace.

Elizabeth at home

Elizabeth and Margaret had a **governess** called Miss Crawford. They called her Crawfie. The princesses did not go to school. Crawfie gave them lessons at home. She also played with them and put them to bed.

Elizabeth was very tidy. For her sixth birthday, she was given a playhouse. It was meant to look like a Welsh cottage. She and Margaret loved cleaning and polishing everything inside.

Elizabeth playing

Elizabeth always loved horses. She got her first pony when she was just three years old. By the time she was ten, she could ride really well.

Elizabeth enjoyed playing outdoors. At weekends her family went walking and cycling in the countryside. They went on holiday to Scotland, where the princesses went swimming at the seaside.

Moving house

When Elizabeth was ten, her father became King. People came to clap and cheer. Elizabeth smiled and waved at the crowds. Later, she wrote a story about the wonderful day.

Elizabeth and her family went to live at
Buckingham Palace. Elizabeth did not
like it because it was big and cold. When
she was 11, she joined the Girl Guides.
She enjoyed being a Guide.

World War Two

When Elizabeth was 13, a war broke out. Many people were killed and no one had enough food. Elizabeth wanted to cheer everyone up. She spoke on the radio to children across the world.

The war was called World War Two. The Army needed young people to help with the war work. When Elizabeth was 19, she joined the Army. She learned to fix cars and drive trucks.

A wedding and a funeral

Elizabeth fell in love with a Navy officer called Prince Philip Mountbatten. They got married in 1947. Their son Charles was born a year later, and their daughter Anne was born in 1950.

Wednesday, February 6, 1952

LATE NIGHT

THE STAR

No. 19,835 ** Three Halfpence

New Queen Flies Home

THE KING DIES IN HIS SLEEP

PRINCESS ELIZABETH, the new Queen, was given the news of her father's death at the Royal lodge at Nyeri, near Nairobi, today. She heard it quietly. Then she broke down and wept.

First picture of the King after his illness at the holiday party for Prince Charles at Buckingham Palace.

THE STORY OF KING GEORGE

Colin Frame tells the full story of the Life of King George—Pages 5, 6, 7, 8 and 9.

The Last Day at Sandringham. — See Star Man's Diary.

The first news to reach the lodge came from a Nairobi newspaper. It was decided to withhold the news from the Princess until direct confirmation was obtained by radio-telephone from the Royal Family in London.

The radio-telephone call was routed to the Princess through a little Kenya country post office.

It took nearly 30 minutes for

CONTINUED ON PAGE TWO

WITH most profound grief the nation learned today that His Majesty The King died peacefully in his sleep early this morning at Sandringham.

The announcement was made from Sandringham at 10.45 a.m.

CONTINUED ON BACK PAGE

Elizabeth and Philip were on holiday in Africa when something very sad happened. Elizabeth's father, the King, suddenly died. This meant that Elizabeth was Queen. She flew back to England at once.

17

Elizabeth is crowned

At her **coronation** in 1953, Elizabeth wore rich robes and sparkling jewels. People all over the world watched on television. This was the first time so many people had seen such an amazing event.

Elizabeth's husband did not change his **title**. He stayed a prince. Their son Andrew was born in 1960, and their son Edward was born four years after that.

The Queen's work

The Queen works hard. She often talks about **government** with the **Prime Minister**. She also goes to events like the Remembrance Sunday **ceremony**, which is to remember people who died in wars. This picture shows her taking part in the parade called **Trooping the Colour**.

Here Queen Elizabeth is **knighting** a man at Buckingham Palace.

Every year, the Queen goes on television to wish everybody Happy Christmas. She sends a birthday card to people who are 100 years old. She also holds ceremonies to **honour** people who have done good work.

Meeting people

The Queen often visits towns and villages in the **UK**. Lots of people wait to see her. She walks about talking to them. Every summer, she holds garden parties for hundreds of her **subjects**.

The Queen travels all over the world to meet leaders of other countries. Sometimes she invites them to Buckingham Palace. She thinks it is important that people everywhere should be friends.

Bad times and good times

In 1992, there was a fire at the Queen's favourite home, Windsor Castle. Many of the things she loved got burned. Then in 1997 Princess Diana, mother of two of the Queen's grandsons, Princes William and Harry, was killed in a traffic accident.

Here, the Queen is looking at the damage caused by the fire.

But the year 2002 was a celebration. It was called Elizabeth's Golden **Jubilee**, because she had been Queen for 50 years. People were happy for her and held parties all over the **UK** and **Commonwealth**.

The Diamond Jubilee

The year 2012 is the Queen's Diamond **Jubilee**. This means that Elizabeth has been Queen for 60 years. Events like this are celebrated all over the world. They are also special for the **royal** family.

Now in her eighties, the Queen is still very busy. Recently she has attended the weddings of three of her grandchildren. The royal family is popular around the world. People love to meet the Queen and her family.

Family tree

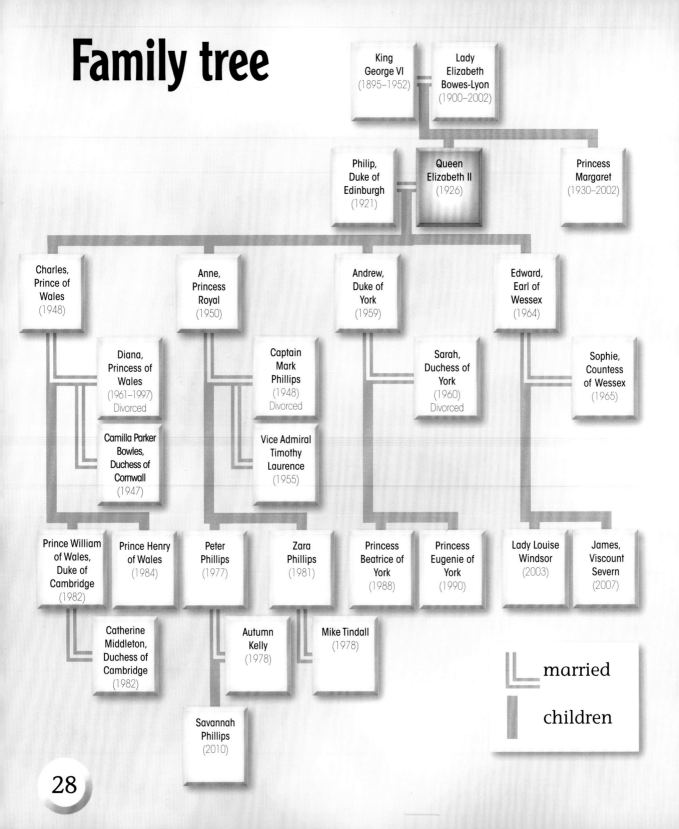

King George VI (1895–1952)

Lady Elizabeth Bowes-Lyon (1900–2002)

Philip, Duke of Edinburgh (1921)

Queen Elizabeth II (1926)

Princess Margaret (1930–2002)

Charles, Prince of Wales (1948)

Anne, Princess Royal (1950)

Andrew, Duke of York (1959)

Edward, Earl of Wessex (1964)

Diana, Princess of Wales (1961–1997) Divorced

Captain Mark Phillips (1948) Divorced

Sarah, Duchess of York (1960) Divorced

Sophie, Countess of Wessex (1965)

Camilla Parker Bowles, Duchess of Cornwall (1947)

Vice Admiral Timothy Laurence (1955)

Prince William of Wales, Duke of Cambridge (1982)

Prince Henry of Wales (1984)

Peter Phillips (1977)

Zara Phillips (1981)

Princess Beatrice of York (1988)

Princess Eugenie of York (1990)

Lady Louise Windsor (2003)

James, Viscount Severn (2007)

Catherine Middleton, Duchess of Cambridge (1982)

Autumn Kelly (1978)

Mike Tindall (1978)

Savannah Phillips (2010)

⌐⌐ married

█ children

Fact file

The Queen's full name is Elizabeth Alexandra Mary Windsor. Her nickname is Lilibet.

The Queen's real birthday is on 21 April, when she celebrates at home with her family. She has an **official** birthday in June, when public celebrations take place.

The Queen owns several homes in the **UK**. The most important ones are Buckingham Palace, Windsor Castle, Sandringham House, and Balmoral Castle.

The Queen does not choose the **Prime Minister** or other people in **government**.

You can see the Queen's picture on money and stamps in **Commonwealth** countries all over the world.

The Queen receives between 200 and 300 letters every day.

When the Queen travels abroad, she takes four and a half tons of luggage. That is even heavier than an elephant!

The Queen has owned dogs called corgis since she was eighteen.

29

Glossary

ceremony special words and actions used at important events

christening ceremony when a new baby is taken to church to give it a name and welcome it into the Christian religion

Commonwealth group made up of countries that were all once ruled by Britain

coronation ceremony when a person is made Queen or King

duchess/duke member of the royal family, next in importance after princess/prince

governess woman who is paid to look after children in their home and to be their teacher

government making decisions and laws for a country. The group of people who do this is also called the government.

honour let someone use a special title

Jubilee when there is a special "birthday" of something that happened

knighting touching a man's shoulders with a sword to honour him with the title 'Sir'

official part of a person's work, and not part of their home life

Prime Minister leader of the government

royal anything to do with a Queen, King, or their family

subject person ruled by a Queen or King

title word used before a name, like Mr, Mrs, Queen, Prince, Duchess

Trooping the Colour parade held to celebrate the Queen's Official Birthday. It means 'marching with the flag'.

United Kingdom (UK) country made up of England, Scotland, Wales, and Northern Ireland

Find out more

Books

Becoming Queen Elizabeth II, G. Clements (Franklin Watts, 2012)

Her Story: Queen Elizabeth II, John Malam (Wayland, 2012)

William and Kate: A Royal Romance, Jane Bingham (Raintree, 2011)

The Ladybird Book of Kings and Queens (Ladybird, 2011)

Websites

www.direct.gov.uk/en/Nl1/Newsroom/DG_197517
The official government website with information on events planned for the Diamond Jubilee.

www.royal.gov.uk
The official website for the Queen and the royal family.

www.thecommonwealth.org
Click on 'Young Commonwealth' to find out about the countries in the Commonwealth.

Places to visit

- Balmoral Castle, Scotland – you can visit an exhibition and you can also go pony-trekking, just like the Queen does.
- Buckingham Palace, London – you can watch the changing of the guard outside. In the summer, you can buy tickets to go inside.
- The Tower of London – the crown jewels are on show in this big castle on the River Thames.
- Westminster Abbey, London – the Queen was crowned and married in this cathedral (big church).
- Windsor Castle, Berkshire – there is a dolls' house here which belonged to the Queen's grandmother when she was young.

Index